George J. Brooke
The Dead Sea Scrolls and German Scholarship

Centrum Orbis Orientalis et Occidentalis (CORO)
Zentrum für Antike und Orient

Akademie der Wissenschaften zu Göttingen
Georg-August-Universität Göttingen

Julius-Wellhausen-Vorlesung

Herausgegeben von
Reinhard G. Kratz und Rudolf Smend

Heft 6

De Gruyter

George J. Brooke

The Dead Sea Scrolls and German Scholarship

Thoughts of an Englishman Abroad

De Gruyter

ISBN 978-3-11-059585-7
e-ISBN (PDF) 978-3-11-059732-5
e-ISBN (EPUB) 978-3-11-059364-8
ISSN 1867-2213

Library of Congress Control Number: 2018944102

Bibliografische Information der Deutschen Nationalbibliothek

Die Deutsche Nationalbibliothek verzeichnet diese Publikation in der Deutschen
Nationalbibliografie; detaillierte bibliografische Daten sind im Internet
über http://dnb.dnb.de abrufbar.

MIX
Papier aus verantwor-
tungsvollen Quellen
FSC® C083411

Inhalt

Grußworte anlässlich des Festakts zum 10-jährigen Bestehen des CORO

Ulrike Beisiegel

Präsidentin der Georg-August-Universität Göttingen

Im Jahr 2015 hat das *Centrum Orbis Orientalis et Occidentalis (CORO)* sein 10-jähriges Bestehen gefeiert. Ich freue mich sehr, dass die Ansprachen und der Hauptvortrag, die anlässlich des damaligen Festakts gehalten wurden, nun in diesem Band versammelt sind und damit für die Öffentlichkeit zur Verfügung gestellt werden.

Das CORO ist auch nach inzwischen über 10 Jahren ein sehr lebendiges Beispiel der engen und erfolgreichen Zusammenarbeit der Georg-August-Universität mit der Göttinger Akademie der Wissenschaften. Es agiert damit nicht nur im Bereich der Forschung integrativ und innovativ, sondern war bei seiner Gründung auch ein erster wichtiger Schritt auf dem Weg zum Göttingen Campus. Inzwischen ist der Göttingen Campus, in dem die Universität mit insgesamt acht außeruniversitären Partnern am Standort zusammenarbeitet, ein in der deutschen Hochschullandschaft fest etablierter Begriff. Vor allem aber ist er ein von den Wissenschaftlerinnen und Wissenschaftlern, aber auch von großen Teilen der Verwaltung täglich gelebtes Prinzip der Kooperation, bei dem die Stärken der einzelnen Partner genutzt werden, um Göttingen gemeinsam als forschungsstarken und lebenswerten Standort weiterzuentwickeln.

Das CORO bringt sich durch die an ihm versammelten Fächer und durch die einzelnen Wissenschaftlerinnen und Wissenschaftler sehr aktiv in die geisteswissenschaftlichen und disziplinübergreifenden Forschungsschwerpunkte der Universität ein, wofür ich allen Mitgliedern herzlich danken möchte. Ich wünsche dem CORO für die nächsten Jahre weiterhin viel Freude an der interdisziplinären Zusammenarbeit und viel Erfolg!

https://doi.org/10.1515/9783110597325-003

Tanja S. Scheer
Direktorin des CORO

Sehr geehrte Frau Präsidentin, liebe Frau Beisiegel,
sehr geehrter Herr Vizepräsident,
sehr geehrte Herren Dekane der theologischen und philosophischen
Fakultät,
sehr geehrter Herr Brooke,
liebe Kolleginnen und Kollegen,
liebe Studierende,
meine Damen und Herren!

Heute begehen wir das 10-jährige Jubiläum dieses Zentrums für Antike und Orient. Es erscheint besonders passend, diesen Festakt mit der Julius-Wellhausen-Vorlesung zu verbinden: Ist diese doch eine inzwischen traditionell gewordene Veranstaltung von CORO und Akademie der Wissenschaften. Wir freuen uns, mit George Brooke einen besonders renommierten internationalen Gelehrten zum Festvortrag bei uns zu haben.

Erlauben Sie mir jedoch, bevor wir ihn hören werden, einige Worte zur Geschichte, zur Arbeit und zu den Zukunftsperspektiven unseres Zentrums für Antike und Orient: Das CORO wurde als Centrum Orbis Orientalis ursprünglich im Jahr 2005 gegründet, die Initiative hierzu kam von Seiten der Theologischen Fakultät: in einem Zentrum für semitische Sprachen sollten auch die „benachbarten Kulturen" beteiligt sein. Im Jahr 2011 schlossen sich die altertumswissenschaftlichen Fächer der Philosophischen Fakultät, die bisher unter dem Kürzel KEMA: „Kulturen Europas und des Mittelmeerraumes in der Antike" (KEMA) einen eigenen Verbund gebildet hatten, mit den schwerpunktmäßig orientalistisch, semitistisch geprägten Fächern des CORO zu einem ganz neuen Verbund zusammen: dies ist unser heutiges Centrum Orbis Orientalis et Occidentalis.

https://doi.org/10.1515/9783110597325-004

Worin liegt die Bedeutung des CORO und welche Ziele verfolgt es im zehnten Jahr seines Bestehens?

Das Centrum versteht sich als Koordinationsplattform und Kompetenzzentrum für die Fächer, die sich mit Geschichte, Sprache, Kunst und Kultur des Mittelmeerraums und des Nahen und Mittleren Ostens befassen. Koordination der Lehre, Unterstützung der Öffentlichkeitsarbeit und Förderung der Forschung in diesen Fächern sind die zentralen Anliegen des CORO.

Bundesweit gesehen greift das CORO eine ganz besondere Stärke der Georg-August-Universität auf: die in Göttingen vorhandene Breite der altertumswissenschaftlichen Fächer. Derzeit sind 19 Fächer im Zentrum vertreten: Das Alte Ägypten bis in die koptische Spätantike, der Alte Orient im Zweistromland und in den Ländern der Bibel, der Vordere Orient und Zentralasien mit Schwerpunkten im alten Persien, im orientalischen Christentum, im arabisch-islamwissenschaftlichen Bereich, sowie in den Kulturen der Turkvölker. Griechenland und Römisches Reich werden im CORO aus historischer, sprachlicher, archäologischer und rechtsgeschichtlicher Perspektive in den Blick genommen, die christliche Spätantike bildet ebenfalls den Schwerpunkt mehrerer beteiligter Fächer und Fachvertreter. Dass es selbst in der breit aufgestellten Göttinger Fachkultur Lücken gibt sei allerdings auch erwähnt: Die Judaistik, aber auch etwa die Vorderasiatische Archäologie sind Fächer, die wir hier vor Ort schmerzlich vermissen. Dennoch: Auf der hier gegebenen und in nur wenigen deutschen Universitäten in gleichem Maße vorhandenen starken Basis der altertumswissenschaftlichen Fächer können wir hier im CORO aufbauen.

Unser interdisziplinäres Zentrum engagiert sich auf mehreren Ebenen für die Koordination von Studium und Lehre: Die Sprachenschule Ludus Linguarum (an der Theologischen Fakultät verortet) koordiniert die Angebote im Bereich der sprachlichen Ausbildung der Studierenden. Für unsere Fächer, in denen oft exotische Sprachen benötigt werden ist das besonders wichtig: So hat das CORO etwa in den letzten Semestern Lehraufträge für das Altäthiopische finanzieren können. Auch die Akademie der Wissenschaften mit ihren Projekten ist in die Lehre des CORO eingebunden: Die Studierenden werden so mit der Arbeitsweise der Grundlagenforschung vertraut gemacht. Schließlich ist das CORO Träger und organisatorischer Überbau von interdisziplinären Studiengängen auf unterschiedlichem Level: Hier liegt die Koordination bei der Philosophischen Fakultät.

Auf Bachelor Niveau gibt der B. A. Antike Kulturen den Studienan-
fängern die Möglichkeit, sich zu Beginn des Studiums in den Fächern
des CORO zu orientieren, und nach Neigung zu kombinieren. Dem aka-
demischen Nachwuchs wird so von Studienbeginn an nicht nur vielfäl-
tiges Wissen, sondern vor allem auch ein interdisziplinärer Blickwinkel
auf die Alte Welt vermittelt. Im CORO-Studiengang wird eine gesamt-
heitliche Perspektive wiederbelebt, die zwischenzeitlich durch die aka-
demische Trennung der Fachkulturen in der deutschen Wissenschaft
schon fast verloren schien. Diese interdisziplinäre Perspektive wird auf
Masterebene weitergeführt, im Master Antike Kulturen – Geschichte
des Altertums. Das Studienangebot Antike Kulturen wird von seiten der
Studierenden sehr gut angenommen: In den vergangenen zwei Jahren
hat sich das Interesse im Vergleich zu den Vorjahren vervierfacht.

Ein zweites Ziel des CORO besteht darin, den orientalistischen und
altertumswissenschaftlichen Fächern größere Sichtbarkeit zu verleihen.
Das betrifft sowohl den Kontext der eigenen Universität, als auch dar-
über hinausgreifend die Öffentlichkeit im größeren Sinne: Die heutige
Julius-Wellhausen-Vorlesung ist hier an herausragender Stelle zu nennen.

Drittens ist die Förderung von Forschungsinitiativen in den beteiligten Fächern ein ganz besonderes Ziel des CORO. Dies geschieht
nicht dirigistisch, sondern aus den Fächern heraus.

Lassen Sie mich hierzu kurz meine ganz persönliche Erfahrung mit
dem CORO beschreiben: Als ich im Jahr 2011 den Lehrstuhl für Alte
Geschichte in Göttingen übernahm, war ich sehr erstaunt zu sehen, wie
intensiv und konstruktiv die altertumswissenschaftlichen Fächer über
die Grenzen der Fakultäten hinweg miteinander im Gespräch waren.
Ganz offensichtlich war es die Zusammenarbeit im Zentrum, die dazu
geführt hatte, dass z. B. die Altorientalistik sich mit der Gräzistik und
Latinistik, aber auch mit den Bibelwissenschaften und der Kirchengeschichte über ‚Mythos' verständigen wollte. Ein noch größerer Kreis
fand sich soeben auf Initiative der älteren Kirchengeschichte zum ge-
meinsamen Thema ‚Bildung und Religion' zusammen. Und man schien
geradezu darauf gewartet zu haben, dass auch mein eigenes Fach, die
Alte Geschichte, sich noch stärker an diesem Gespräch beteiligte:
Das war jedenfalls mein Eindruck als Neuankömmling an der Georg-
August-Universität. Man fand eine Forschungsstruktur vor, auf die man
sich einlassen konnte.

Das CORO gab im Rahmen seiner Möglichkeiten durch gezielte finanzielle Hilfen, aber vor allem als organisatorische Plattform den beteiligten Fächern die Möglichkeit, einzelne Initiativen sichtbar zu machen, gemeinsame Interessenschwerpunkte zu definieren, und sie in gemeinsamer Anstrengung in interdisziplinäre Forschungsvorhaben umzusetzen: Der Erfolg dieses Engagements hat sich in den vergangenen Monaten in einer Reihe neuer Verbundprojekte niedergeschlagen, von denen ich nur zwei nennen will: Den DFG-Sonderforschungsbereich 1136 „Bildung und Religion in Kulturen des Mittelmeerraums und seiner Umwelt" und die DFG-Forschergruppe 2064 „STRATA – Stratifikationsanalysen mythischer Stoffe und Texte in der Antike".

Meine Damen und Herren, wie geht es weiter mit dem Centrum Orbis Orientalis et Occidentalis? Insgesamt hat sich in den letzten Jahren gezeigt: Das CORO als Ganzes – um mit Aristoteles zu sprechen – ist weit mehr als die Summe seiner Teile. Inhaltlich hat sich das CORO auf das Thema ‚Religion' als besonders wichtigen Schwerpunkt für die Zukunft verständigt. Interdisziplinäre Ausbildung von Studierenden weiterzuentwickeln ist ein langfristiges und mühevolles Projekt: unser Promotionsstudiengang Antike Kulturen ist derzeit in Vorbereitung. Öffentlichkeit für unsere Fächer will erst erreicht sein und muss in dauerndem Engagement erhalten bleiben, Verbundprojekte in der Forschung haben lange Vorlaufzeiten. Für diese drei Bereiche brauchen unsere Fächer auch in Zukunft als Basis das Centrum Orbis Orientalis et Occidentalis. Diese Basis ist auch in Zukunft auf die Unterstützung durch das Präsidium und die Fakultäten der Georg-August-Universität dringend angewiesen – auf allen drei genannten Ebenen und nicht zuletzt, wenn es darum geht, konstruktiv über in Göttingen fehlende Fächer nachzudenken.

Besonders zukunftsweisend erscheint allerdings die Expertise aus den soeben gestarteten Verbundprojekten, die das CORO auch in die übergreifenden Forschungsinitiativen der Georg-August-Universität einbringen kann: Wenn es um Clusterbildung geht, um bundesweite Exzellenz, dann wollen und werden die CORO-Fächer mit ihren Ideen, Initiativen und laufenden Projekten dazu beitragen, der Georg-August-Universität im Wettbewerb besondere Überzeugungskraft zu verleihen.

In diesem Sinne wünsche ich dem CORO zum zehnjährigen Jubiläum interdisziplinäre Forschungsideen und deren konstruktive Umsetzung weit über die nächsten zehn Jahre hinaus!

Einführung

Reinhard Kratz

Georg-August-Universität Göttingen

Dear George,
With the ear of an Englishmen abroad you may have been surprised to listen to so many greetings before your lecture starts. The greetings apply to the tenth anniversary of our university centre, *Centrum Orbis Orientalis et Occidentalis*, which is located at the university as well as the academy and is the framework for the *Julius-Wellhausen-Vorlesung* you are invited for. However, the greetings, of course, also apply to you. So, please receive our warm welcome and thank you very much for coming to Goettingen. Before you start, I am afraid that you have to listen to one more greeting, this time introducing you very shortly to the audience. And since the custom of the "Grusswort" is a typical German one, I switch into German, again.

Verehrte Frau Präsidentin,
sehr geehrter Herr Vizepräsident der Akademie,
liebe Frau Scheer,
meine Damen und Herren,

die Idee der *Julius-Wellhausen-Vorlesung* war und ist es, einmal im Jahr renommierte Gelehrte aus dem In- und Ausland nach Göttingen zu locken, die einen Vortrag zu den von Julius Wellhausen repräsentiertem drei Disziplinen – Altes Testament, Arabistik und Neues Testament – oder zu einem angrenzenden Fachgebiet halten. In diesem Jahr ist es uns gelungen, einen Kollegen zu gewinnen, der – ähnlich wie Julius Wellhausen – wenigstens zwei der drei Gebiete, nämlich Altes und Neues Testament, und teilweise auch das dritte, die Semitistik, vertritt: Professor George Brooke, seit 1984 Lecturer, seit 1997 Rylands Pro-

https://doi.org/10.1515/9783110597325-009

fessor of Biblical Criticism and Exegesis in Manchester im Vereinigten Königreich, der Wiege unserer Universität.

Seine Professur teilt den Namen mit der John Rylands Library, die eine der bedeutendsten Sammlungen von antiken Manuskripten und alten Bibeldrucken in Europa beherbergt. Hier ist George Brooke am richtigen Ort, denn er hat schon früh begonnen, sich mit Handschriften zu beschäftigen: Fragmenten aus Qumran oder Dead Sea Scrolls. Nach dem M.A., den er in Oxford erworben hat, und einem PGCE (Post-graduate Certificate of Education) of „the other place", Cambridge, ging George Brooke in die USA, nach Claremont in Kalifornien. Nicht nur, weil es dort sonniger war als in Oxford und Cambridge, sondern weil es ein bedeutendes Zentrum für Handschriften, unter anderem die Handschriften vom Toten Meer, gab. Hier studierte George Brooke bei William Hugh Brownlee, der ihn in die Qumrantexte einführte und für sie gewann, und hier lernte er auch nicht wenige deutsche Kollegen kennen, neben dem Alttestamentler Rolf Knierim auch unseren späteren Göttinger Patristiker, Eckehart Mühlenberg.

Unter der Anleitung von Brownlee verfasste Brooke seine Dissertation „Exegesis at Qumran", die erstmals 1985 publiziert und 2006 noch einmal neu aufgelegt wurde. Es ist ein wegweisendes, die Forschung nachhaltig bestimmendes Buch, das die Hermeneutik und Techniken der Auslegung biblischer Texte in den Schriften von Qumran untersucht und in den Kontext der antiken jüdischen, frühen christlichen (neutestamentlichen) und rabbinischen Auslegung stellt. Hier wird schon die fachliche Breite deutlich, die ihn mit Wellhausen verbindet: mit den Texten vom Toten Meer bewegt man sich zwischen Altem und Neuem Testament und deckt zugleich Bereiche der Judaistik und der Semitistik ab.

Entsprechend breit sind die vielfältigen wissenschaftlichen Aktivitäten, die George Brooke im Laufe seiner Zeit in Manchester seit 1984 entfaltet hat: Er gehört dem internationalen Team der Herausgeber der Handschriften vom Toten Meer in der offiziellen Reihe *Discoveries of the Judaean Desert* an und ist an der Neuedition von Texten beteiligt; er ist Herausgeber der beiden wichtigsten Zeitschriften zu Qumran (*Revue de Qumran* und *Dead Sea Discoveries*, die er mitbegründet hat) sowie Mitherausgeber der Buchreihe *Studies on the Texts of the Desert of Judah*, aber auch Herausgeber des *Journal of Semitic Studies* sowie Mitglied der *Society for Old Testament Study* wie auch der *British Association for Jewish Studies*, in denen er zeitweise den Vorsitz führte.

George Brooke ist auch literarisch überaus produktiv und vor allem innovativ. Wie kein zweiter besitzt er die Fähigkeit, die Qumrantexte in den größeren Kontext der antiken jüdischen und frühchristlichen Literatur, der europäischen und transatlantischen Bibelforschung sowie moderner methodischer Diskurse zu stellen. In diese Richtung geht auch sein Vortrag im Rahmen der Wellhausen-Vorlesung, in dem er den deutschen Beitrag zur Qumranforschung aus der Perspektive der angelsächsischen Forschung, eines „Englishman abroad", betrachtet.

The Dead Sea Scrolls and German Scholarship: Thoughts of an Englishman Abroad

George J. Brooke
University of Manchester

1. Introduction

I am very grateful for the invitation from the Göttingen Akademie der Wissenschaften to contribute to its distinguished series of lectures that honour the memory and immense legacy of Julius Wellhausen. My research world is that of the Dead Sea Scrolls and I can begin by reminding the reader, if reminder is needed, that in some ways from the outset, but especially since 1980, when Professor Hartmut Stegemann was called to be Professor of New Testament, Göttingen has been one of the great world centres for the study of the Dead Sea Scrolls; and since 2002, when the Qumranforschungsstelle was formally instituted here by Professor Reinhard G. Kratz, the study of the Scrolls has blossomed yet further. I have been fortunate enough to have been invited to Göttingen more than once to participate in its many varied, very worthwhile, and long-standing activities and have contributed to several of them (Brooke 2009, 2013, 2016).

What might I have to say to the Akademie and the readers of this study? The most recent, most detailed and highly competent surveys of German Dead Sea Scrolls scholarship have been presented by Jörg Frey (2012), now of the University of Zurich, but also himself a significant contributor to the field when he was in Munich and before that too, and by Annette Steudel (2012), who since her student days and still now represents the long-standing association of Göttingen with the Scrolls.

https://doi.org/10.1515/9783110597325-013

Frey's survey covers many things, but it does not try to locate German Dead Sea Scrolls scholarship within its broader cultural and intellectual contexts; Steudel's essay says more about wider contextual issues and does indeed address several of the topics mentioned in this study, as well as having many details on the involvement of German scholars in the edition of manuscripts for the official series of principal editions, Discoveries in the Judaean Desert (Oxford: Clarendon Press). Nevertheless, despite such comprehensive work, I dare to offer an outsider's view of things and I hope this is both of some value and of some interest as a way of highlighting some of the features of the descriptions by Frey and Steudel, but also as a way of complementing their work.

In my opinion, there are several intertwined features of the intellectual traditions and institutional organisation of German universities that have enabled a distinctive combination of highly significant contributions to the study of the Dead Sea Scrolls. It is difficult to avoid relying upon stereotypes when one attempts to describe intellectual developments in a country where one is a stranger, but this is how the German contributions look to me. My purpose in the published form of this Wellhausen lecture is to reflect briefly on a few aspects of the intellectual history of German-language scholarship on the Dead Sea Scrolls, especially such scholarship within Germany itself. I will also try to develop one or two topics with some examples from my own work on the Scrolls which in several respects has depended upon the work of German scholars. To my mind there are multiple interrelated topics in the discussion, both scholarly and popular, of the Dead Sea Scrolls in Germany and also to some extent in the German diaspora.

Since the era of National Socialism and the Second World War, there have been two great new beginnings in German national life, postwar reconstruction, and the dismantling of the wall with the programme of re-unification. Though it is too simplistic to map German Dead Sea Scroll scholarship directly onto such new beginnings, I am inclined to believe that it is not inappropriate to suggest that there are in some ways two phases of such scholarship as I observe them from outside.

2. The Scrolls and Post-War Reconstruction

The first phase of reconstruction in the immediate post-war period co-incided precisely with the initial discoveries of the scrolls. On 29th November 1947 Eliezer Sukenik (1889–1953) first inspected the Hodayot Scroll (1QHa) and the War Scroll (1QM) on the very day that the United Nations declared the partitioning of Palestine. The first set of new beginnings has allowed for the establishment of Jewish Studies within the German university system in ways that distinguish the German study of Judaism since 1947 from any form of such study that might be described for earlier periods, not least since the scientific study of Judaism in its own right was carried on in many ways outside the universities.

With the creation of the Martin Buber Institut in Cologne, the former student of Kurt Schubert (1923–2007) of Vienna, Johann Maier (b. 1933) developed from 1966 a model centre for Jewish Studies (the second in Germany after the Free University in Berlin; led by Jacob Taubes [1923–1987]) in which the Dead Sea Scrolls played a significant part, not least because of earlier and ongoing collaboration on the Scrolls between Maier and his Doktorvater (Steudel 2012, 565–68). Maier has produced the standard accessible German translation of the Dead Sea Scrolls, in volumes that are now published with various kinds of accompanying data such as lists of scriptural quotations and allusions that are the starting point for any serious reading of the evidence (Maier 1995; Maier and Schubert 1973). It was Maier too who enabled swift access for Germans to the study of the Temple Scroll (11Q19), a text which has had a profound effect in reorienting the study of the Dead Sea Scrolls around the world, even though not so markedly in Germany (Maier 1978). The effect of the Temple Scroll in much study of the Dead Sea Scrolls has been to make discussion of the rewriting of the Torah and legal interpretation of all kinds a priority for the better understanding of various kinds of Jewish movements of the late Second Temple period. However, apart from the somewhat exceptional analysis of Maier, the dominant perspective in German Scrolls scholarship actually remains the prophets and the psalms and their eschatological interpretation in late Second Temple Judaism, rather than attention to the Law in whatever form—and that is a question redolent with the chronological (and even ethical) prioritisations of Wellhausen himself (see e.g., Kratz 2011, 243–71 and 359–79; 2015, 88–104). It is also partly the result of the dominant perspective of New Testament scholars whose study of several parts of the New Testament highlights the ways in which Old Testament prophecies are portrayed as fulfilled in the person of Jesus.

However, for all that the Dead Sea Scrolls played a significant part in the developments of a new kind of Wissenschaft des Judentums, in post-war Germany, so it seems to me, the early powerhouse of Dead Sea Scrolls scholarship was at Heidelberg and the chief instigator of research was Karl Georg Kuhn (1906–1976). Kuhn's personal biography leaves many awkward and unanswered questions (Frey 2012, 532 n. 11), but his stimulation of work on the Dead Sea Scrolls from 1950 onwards cannot be gainsaid and represents a whole set of new beginnings, perhaps for him personally as well as for German New Testament Studies, in which the ways that the Scrolls confirm the character of Judaism at the turn of the era has become a cornerstone of any approach to the Jewishness of Jesus. There are three aspects to Kuhn's leadership and legacy that are probably interwoven but deserve comment because they indicate just how the Dead Sea Scrolls have changed the climate of some parts of Biblical Studies, most especially New Testament Studies, in Germany, in ways that have never been paralleled elsewhere.

The first matter concerns what an outsider might characterise as the German determination to be properly equipped for any task at hand. The fashioning of the proper precision tools for the job has long characterised German craftsmanship at all levels as was especially apparent in a 2014 Exhibition entitled *Germany: Memories of a Nation* at the British Museum which in a central section highlighted the inventive skills of printers, artists, musicians, porcelain makers, metal workers, and precision engineers, amongst several others (MacGregor 2014, 284–375). In the academy the same attention to the production of precision tools is also the case, as Steudel has richly pointed out for the study of the Dead Sea Scrolls (Steudel 2012, 572–75). Of note from Kuhn's research cluster was the production of both the *Rücklaufiges hebräisches Wörterbuch* and the *Konkordanz* of Cave 1 and some Cave 4 texts (Kuhn 1958, 1960). The junior scholars involved in the production of the *Rücklaufiges hebräisches Wörterbuch* were Hartmut Stegemann and Georg Klinzing; those involved in the production of the *Konkordanz* were Albert-Marie Denis, Reinhard Deichgräber, Werner Eiss, Gert Jeremias and Heinz-Wolfgang Kuhn. Both works were standard items in the library of every Scrolls scholar anywhere in the world until replaced by the complete concordances and other tools, especially electronic ones, of recent years. A Qumran *Wörterbuch* is already advertised in the back pages of the 1960 *Konkordanz* and it is a mark of scholarly persistence that the massive undertaking required for such lexicography is now available in its first volume (Kratz, Steudel, and Kottsieper 2017), produced under the auspices of the Akademie der Wissenschaften zu Göttingen.

In fact, alongside Kuhn's precision tool-making other German scholars have also been pre-eminent in equipping the academic world for the task at hand. For example, the assembly of two valuable volumes of partially annotated but exhaustive bibliography by Göttingen native and alumnus Christoph Burchard (b. 1931) distinctively covered both scholarly and popular articles on the Scrolls wherever they might appear, a feat that has not been emulated suitably since (Burchard 1959, 1965). Most worthwhile, but perhaps something of a comparative over-reading of the parallels between the Scrolls and the New Testament, were the rigorously comprehensive volumes produced by Herbert Braun (Braun 1966). Of remarkable value too was Alfred Adam's collection of *Antike Berichte über die Essener* (Adam, 1961), which for over a quarter of a century was the only readily available collection of classical sources for the study of the Essenes. Of importance for introducing generations of students to the texts of the major Scrolls in Hebrew (pointed for beginners) has been Eduard Lohse's (1924–2015) *Die Texte aus Qumran: Hebräisch und Deutsch* (Lohse 1971), the second volume of which was also compiled in Göttingen (Steudel 2001). The Aramaic Scrolls were collected for the first time into a published corpus by Klaus Beyer, whose works have contained ever larger corpora as more manuscripts were published in preliminary or principal editions (Beyer 1984, 1994, 2004).

More than two hundred of the Dead Sea Scrolls from the Qumran caves and several manuscripts from elsewhere in the Judaean wilderness are pre-canonical copies of the books that eventually were included in Jewish and Christian biblical canons. It is those manuscripts, more than anything else, that have stimulated the study of the early history of the transmission of the Hebrew text of the Jewish scriptures, including its Samaritan editions. They have also promoted the study and analysis of the early versions of those scriptures, especially in Greek and Latin. That has come about because the Hebrew manuscripts from the Qumran caves preserve variant readings, both large and small, many of which were known about before 1947, mostly in the versions, but which were commonly understood to be the products of the translators of the texts. Now it is possible to see that in more cases than not, the translators were attempting faithfully to render a form of Hebrew text. The renewed appreciation for the pre-rabbinic history of the transmission of the Hebrew texts of the Jewish scriptures and of their translations into other languages has depended upon the availability of major editions of those texts, all produced in Germany. For standard versions of the Masoretic Text and the Septuagint it is to German institutions and publishing houses that scholars have long turned. And although scholars from other countries have also been involved, the story of dependence on German excellence continues still for Biblica Hebraica Quinta (under the auspices of the German Bible Society; Stuttgart: Deutsche Bibelgesellschaft), the ongoing and pre-eminent Göttingen Septuagint (Göttingen: Vandenhoeck & Ruprecht), the Vetus Latina (sponsored by the Vetus Latina Institute at the Archabbey of Beuron in Baden-Württemberg; Freiburg: Verlag Herder), and now also the Samaritan Pentateuch (at Halle; Berlin: de Gruyter).

Second, Karl-Georg Kuhn is best known in my home institution in Manchester, England, for two smaller matters. On the one hand, on a visit to the Palestine Archaeological Museum in 1953 he was able to peer through the glass of an exhibition case and read enough of the unrolled Copper Scroll to conclude that it was a list of treasure (Kuhn 1954). In 1955 the first roll was cut into strips in Manchester and John Allegro, present at the cutting, became convinced of the correctness of Kuhn's suggestion. Indeed, the correctness of Kuhn's insight as promoted by Allegro has subsequently been confirmed (Brooke 2002). On the other hand, just like Allegro in Manchester, Kuhn enabled the University of Heidelberg to commit funds towards the purchase of some scroll fragments. Whereas no Scrolls ever came to Manchester and the money was returned to the institution, Heidelberg has long been the proud possessor of some fragments of phylacteries which were first published in 1957 (Kuhn 1957) and have recently been re-edited (Busa 2015).

The third matter concerns the way in which Kuhn attracted several young and able researchers who were no doubt excited by the novelty of the Scrolls, but who also were mostly preparing themselves for positions as New Testament scholars. The ability to gather research groups together has been a long-standing advantage of the study of the Humanities in Germany, something that others have tried to copy elsewhere in the world, but not yet with as much success. The doctoral work of Kuhn's set of Scrolls enthusiasts was seen to be part of what was variously becoming to be appreciated as a thorough acknowledgement of and reworking of the Jewish context of Jesus and of the New Testament authors. Some of those scholars have made lifelong contributions in this area (see Frey 2012; Steudel 2012). The landmark series initiated by Kuhn at Heidelberg, Studien zur Umwelt des Neuen Testaments, has included frequently cited monographs by Gert Jeremias (1963), Jürgen Becker (1964), Heinz-Wolfgang Kuhn (1966), Peter von der Osten-Sacken (1969), Georg Klinzing (1971), and Hermann Lichtenberger (1980). Hartmut Stegmann's more popular volume, *Die Essener, Qumran, Johannes der Täufer und Jesus* (Stegemann 1993), stands in the same tradition of providing a wider context, related to the New Testament texts, for understanding the Scrolls from the Qumran caves.

Although the Scrolls from the caves at and near Qumran did indeed merit study in their own right, they were primarily considered in Germany as amazing new data for the understanding of the Umwelt of the New Testament and earliest Christianity. There have been many German Old Testament scholars interested in the Scrolls, at least interested in the text of the scriptural manuscripts, but those scholars with wider research interests in both the Hebrew Bible and the Dead Sea Scrolls have tended to find their academic homes outside Germany itself, as did Odil Hannes Steck (1935–2001) at Zurich or Armin Lange (b. 1961) in Vienna. Lange has been prolific, mostly in English, in the editing of texts, conference volumes, and other resources on the Scrolls, notably a Handbuch on the biblical manuscripts (Lange 2009). The developing research profile of Reinhard Kratz in Göttingen, one of Steck's former students, is the pre-eminent and relatively recent exception that proves the rule, but in general in a striking manner in Germany the wider discourse about the Scrolls has belonged both institutionally and individually with New Testament scholars (Frey 2012, 532–34). That has generally not happened elsewhere, except perhaps with Raymond Brown (1928–1998) and Joseph Fitzmyer (1920–2016) in the United States. I am inclined to think that this is a positive matter. It needs to be recalled that before the Scrolls came to light, all that we had in Hebrew and Aramaic from Palestine of the late Second Temple period were some coin inscriptions, ossuary onomastica, and a few other small items; the Scrolls have changed the landscape fundamentally. In some ways, the discovery of the Scrolls has been one of the principal factors, and a historical one at that, which have limited in German New Testament studies the ongoing influence of Rudolf Bultmann (1886–1976) and his various theological and philosophical agendas and encouraged instead fresh research on the historical Jesus and Judaism of the late Second Temple period (Frey 2012, 535–38). If in Germany the Scrolls had become the exclusive preserve of Old Testament scholars, it is intriguing to wonder where German New Testament scholarship would now be; it would very likely have a rather different character in several respects.

While there might be a slight problem with the way in which some German scholarship has tended to approach the Scrolls, not in their own right, but in order to improve the understanding of Jesus and the New Testament writings, there needs to be some deeper appreciation of the long intellectual context in which such study of the Umwelt has taken and continues to take place. In my opinion, that intellectual context is not narrowly focussed on the figure of Jesus and his first followers, but is characterised by the broad and deep study of religion in antiquity. No other academic tradition has quite produced the equivalent of a Pauly (1796–1845), whose name is synonymous with his edited *Real-Encyclopädie der classischen Alterthumswissenschaft*, whose first volume appeared in 1839, and which has gone through several iterations. Although rooted in the study of the Greek and Roman worlds, this study of religion in antiquity and beyond spread its wings almost from the outset to include what used to be called oriental and Semitic traditions. A similar overarching perspective, but running up to the modern period, is to be seen in *Religion in Geschichte und Gegenwart*, whose first edition appeared in several volumes between 1909 and 1913, and which has also been through several makeovers.

That is the context in which Julius Wellhausen was at home, as his studies of the history of Israelite religion, Christianity and Islam indicate. It is a context of historical studies that might occasionally reflect a tendency towards Romanticism, not least in the identification and interpretation of archaeological remains, as with Heinrich Schliemann (1822–1890) at Troy. But these historical studies are generally to be identified with the currents of German rationalism that in its application to historical issues are more likely sometimes to have tendencies towards historicism, an overly literal reading of the evidence, or towards the over-elaborate reconstruction of the historical development of texts in order to explain their present form. But the primary concern has commonly been with history. "Julius Wellhausen (1844–1918) did not regard the investigation of the composition of the Pentateuch as an end in itself. Rather, it was a means to solving a larger and for him more urgent problem—the history and development of Israelite religion" (Nicholson 1998, 3). "In der Theologie hielt ihn natürlich, nicht die Dogmatik, aber sehr wohl, ihm und der Zeit gemäß, die Geschichte, genauer die biblische Geschichte" (Smend 2004, 12).

This appreciation of religion in antiquity and the classical context very broadly conceived is the background to the work of many German New Testament scholars. For the way in which the Scrolls are part of a broader picture that encourages a redefinition of the way Judaism of the Second Temple period should be understood as Hellenistic Judaism, the work and influence of Martin Hengel (1926–2009) can readily be held up as exemplary, for all that its terms of reference are now being partially redefined yet again. Thus, the Scrolls in the context of German New Testament studies are not simply a convenient purveyor of "background" to the early Christian texts, but to some extent are indeed the arbiters of its various discourses. It is thus no surprise that there are so many volumes on the Dead Sea Scrolls in their own right and concerning their wider implications in both of the Mohr Siebeck series of Wissenschaftliche Untersuchungen zum Neuen Testament, though perhaps especially in the Second Series (e.g., Frey and Popkes 2015); in a notable and striking way, the same is not the case in the Society for New Testament Studies series of Monographs (Cambridge: Cambridge University Press), nor in the Library of New Testament Studies (London: Bloomsbury). A counterpoint to what Mohr Siebeck offers to an audience largely consisting of New Testament scholars has emerged with the publication since 2010 of the *Journal of Ancient Judaism* and its Supplement Series which deliberately aims to set the Scrolls and other Jewish writings from antiquity within a much larger frame of reference (Göttingen: Vandenhoeck & Ruprecht); the very first Supplement is a *Retrograde Hebrew and Aramaic Dictionary* (Sander and Mayerhofer 2010) which provides a much enhanced version of what Kuhn had offered over half a century before. The *Journal of Ancient Judaism* is edited by Maxine Grossman of the University of Maryland and Armin Lange of the University of Vienna.

There is, of course much more to be said about the first period of Scrolls scholarship in Germany, but others have covered thoroughly the principal topics to be associated with the individual contributions of major scholars and all that does not need to be rehearsed again here. It should be noted, however, that several of the trends that are noted above have continued into the second phase of German Dead Sea Scrolls scholarship, not least with the production of immensely valuable scholarly resources as is apparent in the completion of the three-volume *Theologisches Wörterbuch zu den Qumran Texten* (Fabry and Dahmen 2011, 2013, 2016) and the publication of the first volume of the *Hebräisches und Aramäisches Wörterbuch zu den Texten vom Toten Meer* (Kratz, Steudel, and Kottsieper 2017).

3. The Dismantling of the Wall and Thereafter

3.1. The Preliminary Concordance

In Dead Sea Scrolls scholarship a transition began to be felt worldwide in the late 1980s in the constant questioning of restrictions to access of the unpublished fragmentary manuscripts, especially those that came from Qumran's Cave 4 where the largest quantities of material had been recovered, perhaps up to 600 manuscripts in all. The story has been told many times and in many languages. In a recent re-telling by John J. Collins (Collins 2013) there is indeed a brief mention of the important role that a certain concordance played in facilitating access to the unpublished material, but the details of that concordance are not described. A Preliminary Concordance to the Hebrew and Aramaic Fragments from Qumrân Caves II–X Including Especially the Unpublished Material from Cave IV was prepared and arranged for printing by Hans-Peter Richter and states explicitly on its title page that it is distributed by Prof. Dr. Dr. Hartmut Stegemann on behalf of Professor John Strugnell. But, significantly for Göttingen's ongoing role in Dead Sea Scrolls scholarship, this was privately printed in Göttingen and is dated 1988.

In the Preface to the Preliminary Concordance John Strugnell (1930–2007) explained that all the cards were photographed in 1979 thanks to a grant from the Preservation Council of Los Angeles. After that exercise Strugnell tried to reproduce the concordance for himself and his colleagues but noted that whatever kind of technique he used, about thirty per cent of the cards were illegible. The story continued: "In 1985, Hartmut Stegemann made a xerox copy of these films at Göttingen; afterwards, his assistant Hans-Peter Richter came to Jerusalem three times to improve the ca. 2500 sheets of this copy by comparison with the original card-indexes in the Rockefeller Museum. These ventures were generously sponsored by the Akademie der Wissenschaften zu Göttingen, as a support for the future edition of a dictionary to the non-biblical Qumrân texts." The deposit of one copy of the Concordance at the Hebrew Institute for Religion in Cincinnati resulted in its use for the reconstruction of the text of many fragments by Ben-Zion Wacholder and his student Martin Abegg (Wacholder and Abegg 1991, 1992, 1995, 1996). Indirectly and perhaps largely in an unintended manner, the Göttingen Akademie has been responsible for the general release of the scrolls to the world—a splendid achievement. Is it more than a coincidence that the various factors leading to the general liberation of the unpublished Dead Sea Scrolls in 1991 happened at the same time as the manifold political changes that resulted in the demise of the power of the Berlin wall in 1989 and its demolition between 1990 and 1992?

3.2. Manuscript Reconstruction

The reproduction of the Preliminary Concordance was undertaken by Professor Stegemann (1933–2005) because of his long-standing involvement with the scrolls in Jerusalem where he had earned the respect and trust of the members of the team who were editing the unpublished fragmentary manuscripts. His work, as has been very well described by Annette Steudel (Steudel 2012, 583–84; 590–92), involved primarily and where feasible the reconsideration of the allocation of fragments to manuscripts and their placement in relation to each other. That work had borne fruit in the ways that enabled Stegemann to confirm some of the insights of his work on the Hodayot begun in the 1960s in his Heidelberg dissertation (Stegemann 1963) and developed and enhanced in many ways thereafter as elegantly described by Eileen Schuller (Stegemann with Schuller 2009, 13–53).

Hartmut Stegemann's method for the reconstruction of manuscripts is a magisterial contribution to the understanding of the Dead Sea Scrolls from the point of view of their material culture. Here is a facet of the technical excellence of German scholarship at its best; though as a scholar of the Scrolls I have a certain bias, I am inclined to think of the technical expertise that is reflected in the method when properly applied being akin to the incomparable work of the Meissen porcelain factory (cf. de Waal 2015). During a series of summers in Jerusalem Hartmut Stegemann began to train students from various parts of Europe and the United States in his thorough methodological approach. This was most starkly demonstrated in the publication of Carol Newsom's dissertation on the Songs of the Sabbath Sacrifice in 1985, the repeated patterns for some of the manuscript copies being set out as neatly as those of a Bach fugue with diminuendi at each turn and with full acknowledgement of the help given by Stegemann (Newsom 1985, vii–viii).

I first came to learn of Professor Stegemann's approach in an indirect way. In 1987 he graciously accepted my invitation to come to Manchester to attend the International Symposium on the Temple Scroll. He discovered then that my revised doctoral dissertation had been published; in the ensuing conversation he became anxious that I might have pre-empted a project on Eschatological Commentary A (4Q174) to which he had assigned one of his students. I gave him a copy of my book (Brooke 1985). He read it overnight and was delighted, in the kindest way with a sparkle in his eye, to find that my work was somewhat inadequate! Subsequently Annette Steudel was able to apply his method to two related manuscripts (4Q174 and 4Q177) and produce a notable dissertation which is now widely cited as a definitive contribution to the reconstruction and better understanding of smaller, less well-preserved scrolls (Steudel, 1994).

In 1992 I became a member of the increasingly expanding international team of manuscript editors. I travelled to Jerusalem in the summer of 1993 to work on my assignment and learnt first-hand from Professor Stegemann about how to proceed with the fragments allotted to me. Some scholars are inclined to think that his method with the material remains of manuscripts concerns only damage patterns and the intervals between them. But much more was and is involved. Most notably in my case for the principal fragment of Commentary on Genesis A (4Q252), Stegemann advised me as soon as possible to look intently at both sides of the fragment. Such advice seems obvious, but it is still the case that

there are very few images available of the reverse sides of the manuscript fragments from the Qumran caves and elsewhere and a visit to
see the actual fragments is necessary for any scholar preparing an edition of a manuscript. If I had not studied the reverse side of the principal
fragment assigned to me, then I would have missed the most important
clue for the best understanding of the manuscript and its reconstruction.
I had my own Meissen moment! On the back, the verso, were two letters in mirror writing. Without much difficulty, I was able to locate on
the recto of the manuscript the precise place where the letters belonged.
Not only thereafter was it possible to measure precisely the turn of the
manuscript between the recto where the letters belonged and the verso
where they had become stuck, but a whole sequence of other deductions
were swiftly apparent: the fact that the scroll had been rolled very tight-
ly, the strong likelihood that the assigned fragments must have come
from a single sheet of skin since there were no traces of any stitching
or their impression in what remained, and the high probability that the
commentary almost certainly concluded with the interpretation of the
Blessings of Jacob (Brooke 1996, 186–90).

A second technique that Stegemann urged was the making of a fac-
simile model of the proposed manuscript. A preliminary version can
be made from photocopies of one-to-one size images glued to paper in
likely places with margins, columns and lines marked where appropri-
ate. Such a prototype has a thickness not far off that of the prepared skin
as found in many instances, though some scrolls, such as the almost
translucent version of the Temple Scroll (11Q19) are on skin prepared
even more finely. With the remains of what seemed to be a tab at the
very start of the first column, it became apparent that the fragments
assigned to me could be justifiably aligned into six columns of writing
on a single sheet of skin.

Once reconstructed, the reading of the fragments of Commentary
on Genesis A could begin in earnest. There is a problem in the opening
line of column I: "[In] the four hundred and eightieth year of Noah's
life their end (קצם) came for Noah ..." The problem is in the posses-
sive pronominal suffix; it is presented without an antecedent. To what
does "their" refer? The compiler of the Commentary on Genesis A does
not help his reader. The important point to note here is that after the
material remains of the manuscript have been successfully described,
it immediately becomes apparent in column I, line 1, that the text of
the commentary is compiled from several sources. The compiler does

not feel a need to smooth out all the difficulties created because of the way that he selects extracts from his sources to include in his new commentary. The modern reader of the commentary can then proceed with source analysis to try to understand the method of selection of the various sections of comment.

I have applied Stegemann's method to several scrolls, but had most success relatively recently with what has commonly been assumed to be a copy of Genesis (4Q4). The manuscript is extant in a single large fragment that has a striking vertical damage pattern in three places indicating the turn of the scroll when flattened on the floor of the cave, probably in antiquity. Because of the dimensions of the surviving fragment Emanuel Tov (Tov 2005, 98) had already expressed the view that it was unlikely that the manuscript had ever contained the whole of Genesis, but he did not specify how large he thought the manuscript might be. By applying the principles of the Stegemann method of manuscript reconstruction to what can be plainly observed I have argued elsewhere (Brooke 2012) that it is most likely that the manuscript only contained Genesis 1–4 or just possibly Genesis 1–5. This was a surprising discovery to me because I had spent several years working on and writing about the earliest surviving explicit Commentary on Genesis (4Q252) that just happens to begin its engagement with Genesis at Genesis 6.

Are the two manuscripts, 4Q4 and 4Q252, in any way complementary? I am uncertain on this matter though I have already begun to present some preliminary ideas on this in a study in the new German periodical on the Hebrew Bible and Ancient Israel (Brooke 2012a). Two factors might immediately be mentioned as at play in some way. The first is that the opening chapters of Genesis offer a different aetiology for evil than the alternative mythology that might lie behind the text of Genesis 6 and which is reflected in Enochic traditions and the summary narrative of the Noachic and patriarchal period of the Damascus Document (CD II,14–III,1).

> And now, sons, listen to me and I shall open your eyes so that you can see and understand the deeds of God, so that you can walk perfectly on all his paths and not allow yourselves to be attracted by the thoughts of a guilty inclination and lascivious eyes. For many have gone astray due to these: brave heroes stumbled on account of them, from ancient times until now. For having walked in the stubbornness of their hearts the Watchers of the heavens fell; on account of it they were caught, for they did not heed the precepts of God. And their

sons, whose height was like that of cedars and whose bodies were like
mountains, fell. All flesh which there was on the dry earth expired
and they became as if they had never been, because they had realized
their desires and had failed to keep their creator's precepts, until his
wrath flared up against them. Through it, the sons of Noah and their
families strayed, through it, they were cut off (trans. García Martínez
and Tigchelaar 2000, 553).

Here there is neither mention of Adam and Eve, nor of Cain and
Abel. Reference to the first few chapters of Genesis is missing. And
that takes one directly to the second matter, namely that there is relatively little use of material from Genesis 1–5 in the religious literature
most closely associated with the sectarian movement, some small part
of which resided at Qumran for some time in the period before the fall
of the Temple in 70 CE.

In other words, do the observations on the manuscript contents,
which are made more rather than less certain by the application of the
insights of Hartmut Stegemann, permit us to draw larger conclusions
about how Genesis was read by some Jews in the late Second Temple
period? For some readers in antiquity, it seems that to begin reading
Genesis at the equivalent of the start of flood narrative was deemed
most suitable; for others, it was still necessary to engage with the first
few chapters of Genesis, even to read those chapters by themselves
as some kind of corrective to other reading strategies and emphases.
Perhaps the scribe who copied 4QGen^d was determined to provide a
corrective to the generally dominant appeal amongst those with whom
he associated to the Enochic way of thinking.

3.3. Implications for Perennial Questions in Old Testament Scholarship

In those detailed matters in relation to the reading and reception of
Genesis by some Jews in the late Second Temple period it is not clear
that one can discern any of the insights of Wellhausen, of his predeces-
sors or successors. This might indeed be part of the explanation as to
why in general in Germany Old Testament scholars have stayed away
from saying too much about the non-scriptural Dead Sea Scrolls, since
there has not been any extensive interest in the earliest, even pre-canon-

ical, reception of the Scriptural texts. Of course, as mentioned earlier, Old Testament scholars in Germany have certainly long been interested in how the scrolls might contribute to the establishment of the text of the Hebrew Bible. Some of the fascicles of Biblia Hebraica Stuttgartensia attest to the available readings, such as are referred to by David Winton Thomas (1901–1970) for Isaiah or Friedrich Horst (1896–1962) for Qohelet. The ongoing project of Biblia Hebraica Quinta is the valuable creation of an enhanced diplomatic edition with apparatus that includes readings from a wide range of sources: now for Deuteronomy, for example, it is possible to see, with the help of Carmel McCarthey, some of the value of the Temple Scroll for text-critical matters, a fact which to my mind is a very astute contribution to the dismantling of the barriers between so-called lower criticism and its counterpart in higher criticism (McCarthey 2007). As has been pointed out by Rudolf Smend, Wellhausen's first monograph on the text of the Books of Samuel (Wellhausen 1871) encouraged Harry Orlinsky, in the light of some of the information then to hand about Samuel in Hebrew from the Dead Sea Scrolls, to commend Wellhausen as "the most brilliant and penetrating textual critic of the OT" (Smend 2004, 20).

But in the way that authoritative traditions have been transmitted and interpreted in the Scrolls there are hints of literary transmission and development that could well be integrated into what German Old Testament scholarship has continued to struggle with for decades. One topic of ongoing interest concerns the Tetrateuch and the role of Deuteronomy. As with so many things concerning the Dead Sea Scrolls, the evidence does not allow us to make a clear statement about things. Nevertheless, I find it more than intriguing that with the possible exception of the so-called Torah manuscript (4Q365; olim Reworked Pentateuch), there are no manuscripts from amongst the Qumran finds that include the Book of Deuteronomy with its predecessor in the Pentateuch, the Book of Numbers. We have evidence for the presence of Genesis and Exodus on the same scroll (4Q1; 4Q11), as also for Exodus and Leviticus (4Q17), and Leviticus and Numbers (4Q23), but it seems very likely that in the Second Temple period the dominant scribal practice and possibly long-standing scribal tradition was to present Deuteronomy independently from the preceding books. As Wellhausen stated forcefully: "Out of this whole [the Hexateuch], the Book of Deuteronomy, as essentially an independent law-book, admits of being separated most easily" (Wellhausen 1885, 6).

Biblical scholars, most notably amongst them German biblical scholars, have long discussed the double-duty function of the Book of Deuteronomy in some form in the early Second Temple period, namely whether it was the fifth book of a Pentateuch, the first book of the so-called Deuteronomistic History, or a pivotal, even central book in an Enneateuch. Now there is some material manuscript evidence that seems to recognize this in a way which does not force the reader to conclude in favour of one theory or another, but to let the Book of Deuteronomy stand in its multiple usages. It is "an independent law-book."

It is indeed clear from the religious literature from the Qumran caves that the "Law of Moses" was received as five books. In the Damascus Document (CD VIII, 14), for example, a citation of Deuteronomy 9:5 is introduced with "and what Moses said." The phrase "Law of Moses" (e.g., CD XV, 9; XVI, 2; 1QS V, 8) is very likely an idiomatic way of referring to the Pentateuch as a multiple manuscript construct. Its constituent five books might possibly be enumerated in the fragmentary reference to the "boo]ks, divided into five" in 1Q30 1, 4, though the allusion there could just as well be to one particular form of the Books of Psalms. But, despite that evidence, it is also now quite likely that Deuteronomy was also understood as a law apart. The way in which the text of Deuteronomy, especially the so-called "Law for the Land" (Deuteronomy 12–26), is distinctly respected in the Temple Scroll (cols LI–LXVI) seems to support such an interpretation. In addition, a compilation of authoritative scriptural extracts such as the Testimonia document (4Q175), cites Exodus, Numbers, Deuteronomy, and Joshua, all in particular text traditions in what we might take as a recognized, authoritative or "canonical" order, reflecting a Hexateuch, or at least a hexateuchal appreciation of the order and relation of the texts with one another (see Lucassen 1998; Römer 2013, 20–22). Indeed, the existence amongst the Scrolls of several rewritten or updated forms of Joshua, as for the books of the Torah themselves, indicates that the book probably had a status not unlike that of the books of the Torah. All of that needs to be taken into account in any reconsideration of Wellhausen on the Hexateuch (see Smend 1999, 630) and those who have developed his ideas: "The five Books of Moses and the Book of Joshua constitute one whole, the conquest of the Promised Land rather than the death of Moses forming the true conclusion of the patriarchal history, the exodus, and the wandering in the wilderness. From a literary point of view, accordingly, it is more accurate to speak of the Hexateuch than the Pentateuch" (Wellhausen 1885, 6). The existence of all the former prophets, the historical books, on one scroll in the Dead Sea collection has been suggested too, but this, it seems to me is unlikely (Trebolle Barrera 1995, 179–83).

As for the Torah and related books, so for the literary Prophets. In the Great Isaiah Scroll (1QIsaᵃ) the three-line blank space at the bottom of Column XXVII is also the end of Isaiah 33. Something of the significance of this was first extensively discussed by Paul Kahle (Kahle 1951, 72–77), Martin Noth (Noth 1951, 224–26) and Curt Kuhl (Kuhl 1952, 332–33) in various German studies, but none of them had the evidence of the Cave 4 manuscripts of Isaiah available to them. That evidence now strongly indicates that in the Second Temple period Isaiah was copied in two halves, since the majority of Cave 4 Isaiah manuscripts contain either the first half or the second half of the book. Such practice resonates with the comment in Josephus that Isaiah's prophecies were "left behind in books" (*Ant.* 10.35). To my mind much could be learnt from a thorough investigation of all the manuscripts of Isaiah according to the principles of reconstruction associated with Hartmut Stegemann; perhaps a German or more specifically a Göttingen project could be initiated to undertake this.

Whatever the case with the fragments assigned to the various manuscript copies of Isaiah, it is also remarkable that the earliest interpretative tradition seems to endorse this transmission practice as not just a scribal convenience, but also as conveying some meaning. All but one of the Isaiah pesharim from the Qumran caves interpret passages either just from the first half of the book or just from the second half. The one exception, Commentary on Isaiah E (4Q165), has several distinctive features and may be alluding to Isaiah 40:12 as a subsidiary reference within a commentary that covers in brief in its extant parts Isaiah 14–32. Or again, the much-discussed so-called Messianic Apocalypse (4Q521), describes divine activity in the eschatological age through a combination of Isaiah 35, Isaiah 61, and various Psalms, in a way that has also been suggested for the response of Jesus to John's disciples according to Luke 7:22–23 (a combination of Isa 35:5–6 and Isa 61:1). In other words, although Isaiah was known in its entirety as a complete work, its interpretation in antiquity might reflect an understanding of its two-part transmission. Peter Höffken has noted that bisection of Isaiah has been widely mentioned but not developed by Isaiah commentators (Höffken 2004, 131–32). I sometimes wonder whether it is time to move away from the norm for appreciating the composite nature of Isaiah set by the Göttingen alumnus Bernhard Duhm (1847–1928) in 1892 to a view such as is instinctively represented in *Ein deutsches Requiem* of the 1860s. In the second movement of the *Requiem* Johannes Brahms (1833–1897), who was his own librettist, sets Isaiah 40:6–9 (1 Peter 1:24–25) in inclusio sequence with James 5:7 before reaching a climax in the magisterial chorus that uses the words of Isaiah 35:10.

Those are some of the implications of working with the material evidence of the scrolls, a few comments restricted largely to the so-called biblical scrolls.

3.4. Further Technical Work

The enviable technical expertise of German institutions goes beyond that of the kinds of tools represented by concordances and dictionaries and beyond the application of reconstruction theories as outlined and honed over many years by Stegemann and those who were fortunate enough to be trained by him. Through a fortuitous set of circumstances, I was able to secure for the John Rylands Library in Manchester the set of fragments that had been variously sent for the analysis of their collagen to Ronald Reed, a Manchester graduate and world-renowned leather expert, who had a position in the Leather Department at the University of Leeds. Through magnification Reed was able to look at the collagen chains of the skin and suggest a date that might reflect such deterioration; that confirmed independently dates provided by palaeographical analysis and carbon14. After Reed's death his family, also Manchester graduates, began to sort through his possessions and discovered the scroll fragments in the loft of the family home.

The Reed family allegiance to Manchester and several chance encounters not only brought the fragments to Manchester, but also enabled ongoing cooperation between Manchester and the Bundesanstalt für Materialforschung und -prüfung (BAM) in Berlin. Dr. Ira Rabin, an Israeli scientist affiliated to BAM, has encouraged the development of interest there in the three-dimensional synchrotron based X-ray fluorescence analysis of several fragments (see the press release: http://www.bam.de/en/aktuell/aktuelle_meldungen/ qum-

ran.htm). Whereas much of the analysis of pottery and other artefacts
has taken place in Israel, especially in Jerusalem, the archaeometry of
the scrolls themselves is taking place especially in Germany, in Berlin.
In addition to preliminary work on samples from the Manchester Reed
Collection of fragments, analysis has also been undertaken on several
of the fragments in the collection of Martin Schøyen, some of which
were purchased from the family of John Trever (Rabin 2016). Trever
had acquired some small fragments from the scrolls from Cave 1 that
had been brought to the American School of Oriental Research (now
the Albright Institute) in February 1948. The spectrometric data available through the analysis of many of these fragments in Berlin is providing new information about the chemical composition of the manuscript sheets and the inks used on them. The results of the analysis have
yet to be tested more widely, but some of the implications of the work
will impinge on the better understanding of where some of the animals
lived, on the processes and places of the production of sheets of skin,
and on the character of the ink used. "Vorsprung durch Technik," a 1982
slogan for which a British advertising agency was responsible, certainly
seems to apply. BAM continues to play a part in the analysis of fragments which have come on to the market since 2002.

3.5. Rethinking the Construction of Judaism in the Late Second Temple Period

Beyond the way that Stegemann's method of reconstruction has opened
up several new avenues of research, attention also needs to be given
to his popular work on the Scrolls (Stegemann, 1993), which together
with a few other introductory texts, is a standard way into the study of
the Scrolls for Germans, amateurs and professionals alike. Although
written to provide a counter-argument to various sensational and
best-selling works, I think that Stegemann's book has yet to be properly
understood as a contribution to what I have described earlier, namely
the study of religion in antiquity, which in my opinion is the major
intellectual context into which the Scrolls are seen to take their place.
At the Madrid conference on the Dead Sea Scrolls, Stegemann first
presented his ideas on the very wide presence of the Essene "Union," as

he called it (Stegemann 1992). He was amongst the first to open up the likelihood that what the Scrolls represent is an alternative way of constructing religion in Palestine in late Second Temple times, a construction which would automatically include the nascent Jesus movement, not because the Scrolls proved that Jesus was an Essene and Paul's hidden years were spent with the Damascus Covenanters, but because phenomenologically a relatively small area for whatever reasons was producing strands of reformation, even innovation, whose roots could be traced back centuries. As the labours of Martin Hengel on Judaism and Hellenism continue to have influence, so the contribution of Hartmut Stegemann to setting the Scrolls in its wider context needs proper and suitable acknowledgment. Twenty years later most scholars are now attentive to the wider cultural contexts of the Scrolls, whether in terms of small group activity, or the production of pottery and other artefacts, or the development of authoritative texts and explicit interpretative approaches to them, or the calculations of calendars and priestly courses, or the practice of medicine, or the use of prayer and apotropaic practices, even manuscript production and the use of papyrus. The full publication of the archaeological remains from the Qumran site is likely to endorse this view.

3.6. The Scrolls and the German Public

If Stegemann's popular book was written in part to help construct the public imagination concerning the Scrolls and their significance, then it is important for Dead Sea Scrolls scholars to engage with the wider public in a positive manner. Christoph Burchard's bibliographies took note of the popular articles generated in the first decade or more after the discovery of Cave 1. There are, perhaps unfortunately, two sides to this. As mentioned earlier, the influence of German rationalism and the pre-occupation with historical reconstruction, of which Wellhausen is a renowned and still influential example for all the right reasons, can nevertheless lead to some overstatements and unfortunate historicism. In fact, Hartmut Stegemann himself in his unpublished but widely circulated Bonn Dissertation of 1965 sometimes pushed the evidence as far as it will go, even too far (Stegemann 1971). The dissertation remains a widely used source for the range of information that needs to be considered, but too much seems to be read off the surface of the texts, especially the Qumran texts. Similar concerns with more detailed historical reconstruction than the texts actually permit can be found, for example, in the works of Hans Burgmann (1986, 1987).

Much more problematic historically are works such as those of Carsten Peter Thiede (1952–2004) which insist on the presence of a fragment of Mark in Cave 7 (Thiede 1986) and the Essenes as a missionary movement (Thiede 2002). Several other German Bible enthusiasts could be mentioned here too; it is not necessary to name such writers and their works, but it is worth remarking on what they represent phenomenologically. There is a sense in the works of Thiede and others that the romanticism that can be felt when there is a tangible connection with the world of the period of Jesus permits ambitious historical reconstruction; however, the actual case is that most commonly more is said than can be said. I think that there could well be a place here for a sophisticated up-to-date study that might take as its starting point Georg Simmel's (1858–1918) landmark essay concerning the romantic fascination with ruins (Simmel 1907). Troy, Stonehenge and Qumran have all suffered similarly at the hands of some experts and in the popular imagination: to prevent the collapse into nature, the historian reads reconstruction into the ruin and risks creating an imaginary world. Perhaps with sensitivity to that problem it is notable that there have been German initiatives to engage not just in some theoretical reflection on the archaeology of the Qumran site and how it has been studied (Rohrhirsch 1996), but also in the analysis of the site and its context (Frey, Claussen and Kessler 2011).

But alongside the tendency towards historicism and the over-enthusiastic historical reconstructions and their ramifications must be put the more positive aspects of popular enthusiasm for the Scrolls. Such a positive perspective might be best represented in the enthusiasm of Alexander Schick (b. 1962). In his books and with his exhibitions he has attempted to engage the German popular imagination in a responsible fashion (Schick 1996, 2000). Some might disagree with his approach, but he has tried to integrate the views of established scholars into his presentations as the use of their names on his title pages indicates. In fact, because of his desire to put artefacts and replicas before the German public and because of his concern to re-present the enthusiasm of the first generation of scholars, Schick has become the repository for the legacy of Claus-Hunno Hunzinger (b. 1929). An alumnus of Göttingen, Hunzinger studied under Joachim Jeremias (1900–1979) and through the assistance of Martin Noth came in October 1954 to be the German representative on the editorial team assembled by Roland de Vaux to cope with the thousands of Cave 4 fragments. Hunzinger subsequently withdrew from this role and his responsibilities were passed to Maurice Baillet. Hunzinger's legacy rests in the popular presentation of his interests by others.

Such popular fascination in Germany with the Dead Sea Scrolls is supported by a wide range of reliable publications. A highly illustrated introduction to the Scrolls can be found in the German translation of *The Complete World of the Dead Sea Scrolls* (Davies, Brooke and Callaway 2002). More recently, replacing James VanderKam's *Einführung* (VanderKam 1998), highly readable but scholarly introductory guides to the Dead Sea Scrolls have become available, resources which deserve circulation well beyond German-speaking communities (Xeravits and Porzig 2015; Stökl Ben Ezra 2016). Somewhat more technical, but nevertheless accessible to those with introductory knowledge are the collections of essays in the Einblicke series (e.g., Frey and Stegemann 2003; Dahmen, Stegemann and Stemberger 2006; Frey and Becker 2007).

3.7. The Göttingen Qumran-Forschungsstelle

The Qumranforschungsstelle was founded in Heidelberg, but came with Hartmut Stegemann by way of Marburg to Göttingen. Dead Sea Scrolls research is continuing to flourish at Göttingen. Reinhard Kratz, as a leading Old Testament scholar, has for several years now been encouraging both Old and New Testament scholars to pay more attention to the Scrolls. He has published widely on multiple biblical topics seen freshly from a Scrolls perspective, but a key measure of his concern with re-introducing Old Testament colleagues to the Scrolls is the way that as an editor of the series Beihefte zur Zeitschrift für die alttestamentliche Wissenschaft (Berlin: de Gruyter) he has welcomed into the series with his co-editors monographs and collections of essays that deal directly with the Dead Sea Scrolls, especially what might be deemed to be the non-sectarian or pre-sectarian ones (see e.g., Kratz and Dimant 2013).

In addition, as Annette Steudel has pointed out, Kratz's direction of the Göttingen Qumranforschungsstelle has seen a shift away from concern with the Umwelt of Jesus and the New Testament towards a concern to engage with the Scrolls with all the literary tools of German Old Testament scholarship, especially redaction criticism (Steudel 2012, 598). This is having some effect in the understanding of the literary composition of various sectarian compositions and their relationships to one another (Kratz 2011). But beyond that there is a view emerging of "a genuine connection between the Qumran group and biblical Judaism"; "biblical Judaism provided a foundation for the community at Qumran, but the two cannot simply be equated. Rather, Qumran represents an advanced yet radicalised stage of biblical Judaism" (Kratz 2013, 220–21; ET 2015, 164–65). Though the label "biblical Judaism" might be queried, what is beginning to emerge is the possibility both of reading the biblical evidence forward and also the Qumran evidence backwards. This is the possibility for creating a meaningful set of historical trajectories which requires sophisticated handling of the evidence; straight lines of dependence should not be drawn too quickly but the contribution of the Dead Sea Scrolls to the better appreciation of the transmission of traditions in the Second Temple period has been recognized in new and invigorating ways. Most likely, because of its material basis and its historical potential, Wellhausen would have been captivated by the possibilities of such a project.

Through multiple publications, not least the first volume of *Hebräisches und aramäisches Wörterbuch zu den Texten vom Toten Meer, einschließlich der Manuskripte aus der Kairoer Geniza*, a new era in the study of the Scrolls in Germany is emerging.

4. Conclusion: From the Present into the Future

It is clear that the German contribution to Dead Sea Scrolls scholarship in the years to come will continue to be very considerable.

First, there is text and the tools needed for reading it. Deep within the Lutheran attitude is attention to the text and its reception: "Christ's kingdom is a hearing-kingdom, not a seeing-kingdom; for the eyes do not guide and lead us to where we find and come to know Christ, but rather the ears do this" (Luther, *Sermon delivered at Merseburg*). This move towards the primacy of text in the Reformation period is part and parcel of a number of cultural shifts of that time. But in Germany attention to ancient texts and the means for their proper excavation remains paramount. All kinds of tools, especially electronic ones are still required for the study of the Scrolls, from new editions to analytical tools, including the Göttingen *Wörterbuch*. All this, as Wellhausen stressed, has initially a historical context and purpose before it has wider implications for various modern cultural contexts. Within such a historical perspective, it would be good to see before too long a reference to a variant in a scriptural manuscript amongst the Dead Sea Scrolls in the marginalia or footnotes of the *Novum Testamentum Graece*, just as they can be found in critical editions of the Hebrew Bible and its versions.

Second, in the last decade or more a significant interest has emerged in reception history and since the Scrolls represent much of the earliest reception of the biblical traditions, they can be understood as having some pre-eminence in making a prominent contribution to how all texts are receptions each in their own generations, from the earliest sources through what we anachronistically perceive to be various re-writings. All is Fortschreibung, ongoing updating; and that does not take place in straightforward and simple ways, but with all the complexity of oral-written interactions and multiple intertextualities, implicit and explicit, verbal and non-verbal.

Third, it is intriguing that in German Dead Sea Scrolls scholarship, and in German biblical scholarship more widely, there is general resistance to the application of novel or contemporary reading strategies (e.g., Dreytza, Hillbrands and Schmid 2002). For example, even long-standing theories on sectarianism or denominationalism are sidelined in preference for discussion of classical associations. The dominant voice is one of the history of religions, and of concomitant historical criticism. That being so, there is room for a German project in Formgeschichte that might collect literary forms in the Scrolls. This might be done in a way similar to that undertaken for the Hebrew Bible under the inspiration of Gerhard von Rad and others in the Forms of the Old Testament Literature series (Grand Rapids: Eerdmans). That might be particularly instructive, if the right kind of comparative data from the ancient world is also included. But certainly, as is already the case in Göttingen, much attention can be paid to the thorough application of redaction criticism to the better-preserved Scrolls and their multiple versions or editions.

Fourth, alongside the writings of Gerhard von Rad, a generation of students of the Hebrew Bible in the Western world have been brought up on Walther Eichrodt's *Theology*. Since the Reformation it has been German voices that have produced the finest systematic theologies, not least in Biblical Studies. For the authors of the Scrolls, God and the world of spirits were an ongoing reality of righteous mercy and compassion, on the one hand, and threat, on the other. How should that be articulated now? It is well-known that the English are suspicious of biblical theology, but some attempt at a synthesis of the world views represented in the sectarian Scrolls at least seems worthwhile. Bonn's *Theologisches Wörterbuch zu den Qumrantexten* could be understood as a step in the right direction but, for all its worthiness in word studies, it does not give access to the spiritual realities of Jewish antiquity. Here is a task for a German Dead Sea Scrolls specialist.

In Göttingen, in Wilhelmsplatz, there is of course a fine statue of William IV, whose benign reign from a distance in Britain was appreciated by many of his subjects in the Electorate of Hanover. I hope that these few comments from a similar distance will be treated as equally benign.

Bibliography

Adam, Alfred. 1961. *Antike Berichte über die Essener.* Berlin: de Gruyter.

Becker, Jürgen. 1964. *Das Heil Gottes: Heils- und Sündenbegriffe in den Qumran-texten und im Neuen Testament.* Studien zur Umwelt des Neuen Testaments 3. Göttingen: Vandenhoeck & Ruprecht.

Beyer, Klaus. 1984. *Die aramäischen Texte vom Toten Meer samt den Inschriften aus Palästina, dem Testament Levis aus der Kairoer Genisa, der Fadenrolle und den alten talmudischen Zitaten.* Göttingen: Vandenhoeck & Ruprecht.

———. 1994. *Die aramäischen Texte vom Toten Meer samt den Inschriften aus Palästina, dem Testament Levis aus der Kairoer Genisa, der Fadenrolle und den alten talmudischen Zitaten.* Ergänzungsband. Göttingen: Vandenhoeck & Ruprecht.

———. 2004. *Die aramäischen Texte vom Toten Meer samt den Inschriften aus Palästina, dem Testament Levis aus der Kairoer Genisa, der Fadenrolle und den alten talmudischen Zitaten.* Band 2. Göttingen: Vandenhoeck & Ruprecht.

Braun, Herbert. 1966. *Qumran und das Neue Testament.* I–II. Tübingen: J. C. B. Mohr [Paul Siebeck].

Brooke, George J. 1985. *Exegesis at Qumran: 4QFlorilegium in its Jewish Context.* Journal for the Study of the Old Testament Supplement 29. Sheffield: JSOT Press.

———. 1996. "Commentaries on Genesis and Malachi." Pp. 185–36 in *Qumran Cave 4.XVII: Parabiblical Texts, Part 3.* Ed. James VanderKam et al. Discoveries in the Judaean Desert 22. Oxford: Clarendon Press.

———. 2002. "Introduction." Pp. 1–9 in *Copper Scroll Studies.* Ed. George J. Brooke and Philip R. Davies. Journal for the Study of the Pseudepigrapha 40. London: Sheffield Academic Press; repr. London: T & T Clark International, 2004.

———. 2009, "New Perspectives on the Bible and its Interpretation in the Dead Sea Scrolls." Pp. 19–37 in *The Dynamics of Language and Exegesis at Qumran.* Ed. Devorah Dimant and Reinhard G. Kratz. Forschungen zum Alten Testament 2/35. Tübingen: Mohr Siebeck.

———. 2012. "4QGen^d Reconsidered." Pp. 51–70 in *Florilegium Complutense: Textual Criticism and Dead Sea Scrolls Studies in Honour of Julio Trebolle Barrera.* Ed. Andres Piquer Otero and Pablo A. Torijano Morales. Journal for the Study of Judaism Supplement 158. Leiden: Brill.

———. 2012a. "Genesis 1–11 in the Light of Some Aspects of the Transmission of Genesis in Late Second Temple Times." *Hebrew Bible and Ancient Israel* 1/4: 465–82.

———. 2013. "Jacob and His House in the Scrolls from Qumran." Pp. 171–88 in *Rewriting and Interpreting the Hebrew Bible: The Biblical Patriarchs in the Light of the Dead Sea Scrolls.* Ed. Devorah Dimant and Reinhard G. Kratz.

https://doi.org/10.1515/9783110597325-039

Beihefte zur Zeitschrift für die alttestamentliche Wissenschaft 439. Berlin: de Gruyter.

———. 2016. "Isaiah in Some of the Non-Scriptural Dead Sea Scrolls." Pp. 243–60 in *Transmission and Interpretation of the Book of Isaiah in the Context of Intra- and Interreligious Debates*. Ed. Florian Wilk. Bibliotheca Ephemeridum Theologicarum Lovaniensium 280 (Leuven: Peeters).

Burchard, Christoph. 1959. *Bibliographie zu den Handschriften vom Toten Meer.* Beihefte zur Zeitschrift für die alttestamentliche Wissenschaft 76. Berlin: Alfred Töpelmann.

Burchard, Christoph. 1959. *Bibliographie zu den Handschriften vom Toten Meer.* Bd. II. Beihefte zur Zeitschrift für die alttestamentliche Wissenschaft 89. Berlin: Alfred Töpelmann.

Burgmann, Hans. 1986. *Zwei lösbare Qumrânprobleme: Die Person des Lügenmannes, die Interkalation im Kalendar*. Frankfurt: Peter Lang.

———. 1987. *Vorgeschichte und Frühgeschichte der essenischen Gemeinden von Qumrân und Damaskus*. Arbeiten zum Neuen Testament und Judentum 7. Frankfurt: Peter Lang.

Busa, Anna. 2015. *Die Phylakterien von Qumran (4Q128.129.135.137) aus der Heidelberger Papyrussammlung*. Veröfflichungen aus der Heidelberger Papyrus-Sammlung, Neue Folge. Herausgegeben von der Heidelberger Akademie der Wissenschaften. Philosophisch-historische Klasse 15. Heidelberg: Universitätsverlag Winter.

Collins, John J. 2013. *The Dead Sea Scrolls: A Biography*. Lives of Great Religious Texts. Princeton: Princeton University Press.

Dahmen, Ulrich, Hartmut Stegemann and Günter Stemberger (eds). 2006. *Qumran – Bibelwissenschaften – Antike Judentum*. Einblicke 9. Paderborn: Bonifatius.

Davies, Philip R., George J. Brooke and Phillip R. Callaway. 2002. *Qumran: Die Schriftrollen vom Toten Meer*. Trans. T. Bertram. Stuttgart: Theiss and Wissenschaftliche Buchgesellschaft.

Dreytza, Manfred, Walter Hillebrands and Hartmut Schmid. 2002. *Das Studium des Alten Testaments: Eine Einführung in die Methoden der Exegese*. Bibelwissenschaftliche Monographien 10. Wuppertal: Brockhaus.

Fabry, Heinz-Josef, and Ulrich Dahmen (eds). 2011. *Theologisches Wörterbuch zu den Qumrantexten. Band I.* Stuttgart: Kohlhammer.

Fabry, Heinz-Josef, and Ulrich Dahmen (eds). 2013. *Theologisches Wörterbuch zu den Qumrantexten. Band II.* Stuttgart: Kohlhammer.

Fabry, Heinz-Josef, and Ulrich Dahmen (eds). 2016. *Theologisches Wörterbuch zu den Qumrantexten. Band III.* Stuttgart: Kohlhammer.

Frey, Jörg, and Hartmut Stegemann (eds). 2003. *Qumran kontrovers: Beiträge zu den Textfunden vom Toten Meer*. Einblicke 6. Paderborn: Bonifatius.

Frey, Jörg, and Michael Becker (eds). 2007. *Apokalyptik und Qumran*. Einblicke 10. Paderborn: Bonifatius.

Frey, Jörg. 2012. "Qumran Research and Biblical Scholarship in Germany." Pp. 529–564 in *The Dead Sea Scrolls in Scholarly Perspective: A History of Research*. Ed. Devorah Dimant. Studies on the Texts of the Desert of Judah 99. Leiden: Brill.

Frey, Jörg, and Enno Edzard Popkes (eds). 2015. *Jesus, Paulus und die Texte von Qumran*. Wissenschaftliche Untersuchungen zum Neuen Testament 2/390. Tübingen: Mohr Siebeck.

García Martínez, Florentino, and Eibert J. C. Tigchelaar. 2000. *The Dead Sea Scrolls Study Edition*. 2 Volumes. Leiden: Brill; Grand Rapids, MI: Eerdmans.

Höffken, Peter. 2004. *Jesaja: Der Stand der theologischen Diskussion*. Darmstadt: Wissenschaftliche Buchgesellschaft.

Jeremias, Gert. 1963. *Der Lehrer der Gerechtigkeit*. Studien zur Umwelt des Neuen Testaments 2. Göttingen: Vandenhoeck & Ruprecht.

Kahle, Paul. 1951. *Die hebräischen Handschriften aus der Höhle*. Stuttgart: Kohlhammer.

Klinzing, Georg. 1971. *Die Umdeutung des Kultus in der Qumrangemeinde und im Neuen Testament*. Studien zur Umwelt des Neuen Testaments 7. Göttingen: Vandenhoeck & Ruprecht.

Kratz, Reinhard G. 2011. *Prophetenstudien: Kleine Schriften II*. Forschungen zum Alten Testament 74. Tübingen: Mohr Siebeck.

———. 2011. "Der *Penal Code* und das Verhältnis von *Serekh ha-Yachad* (S) und *Damaskusschrift* (D)." *Revue de Qumrân* 25: 199–227.

———. 2013. *Historisches und biblisches Israel: Drei Überblicke zum Alten Testament* (Tübingen: Mohr Siebeck). Revised and enlarged in ET: *Historical and Biblical Israel: The History, Tradition, and Archives of Israel and Judah*. Oxford: Oxford University Press, 2015.

———., and Devorah Dimant (eds). 2013. *Rewriting and Interpreting the Hebrew Bible: The Biblical Patriarchs in the Light of the Dead Sea Scrolls*. Beihefte zur Zeitschrift für die alttestamentliche Wissenschaft 439. Berlin: de Gruyter.

———. 2015. *The Prophets of Israel*. Trans. Anselm Hagedorn and Nathan MacDonald. Critical Studies in the Hebrew Bible 2. Winona Lake, IN: Eisenbrauns.

Kratz, Reinhard G., Annette Steudel, and Ingo Kottsieper (eds). 2017. *Hebräisches und aramäisches Wörterbuch zu den Texten vom Toten Meer, einschließlich der Manuskripte aus der Kairoer Geniza. Band 1* ב–א (Berlin: de Gruyter)

Kuhl, Curt. 1952. "Schreibereigentümlichkeiten: Bemerkungen zur Jesajarolle (DSIa)." *Vetus Testamentum* 2: 307–33.

Kuhn, Heinz-Wolfgang. 1966. *Enderwartung und gegenwärtiges Heil: Untersuchungen zu den Gemeindeliedern von Qumran*. Studien zur Umwelt des Neuen Testaments 4. Göttingen: Vandenhoeck & Ruprecht.

Kuhn, Karl Georg. 1954. "Les rouleaux de cuivre de Qumrân." *Revue Biblique* 61 (1954): 193–205.

———. 1957. *Phylakterien aus Höhle 4 von Qumran*. Abhandlungen der Heidelberger Akademie der Wissenschaften. Philosophisch-historische Klasse 1957/1. Heidelberg: C. Winter.

Kuhn, Karl Georg, et al. 1958. *Rückläufiges Hebräisches Wörterbuch; Retrograde Hebrew Lexicon*. Göttingen: Vandenhoeck & Ruprecht.

Kuhn, Karl Georg, et al. 1960. *Konkordanz zu den Qumrantexten*. Göttingen: Vandenhoeck & Ruprecht.

Lange, Armin. 2009. *Handbuch der Textfunde vom Toten Meer. Band 1: Die Handschriften biblischer Bücher von Qumran und den anderen Fundorten*. Tübingen: Mohr Siebeck.

Lichtenberger, Hermann. 1980. *Studien zum Menschenbild in Texten der Qumrangemeinde*. Studien zur Umwelt des Neuen Testaments 15. Göttingen: Vandenhoeck & Ruprecht.

Lohse, Eduard. 1971. *Die Texte aus Qumran: Hebräisch und Deutsch*. München: Kösel-Verlag.

Lucassen, Birgit. 1998. "Josua, Richter und CD." *Revue de Qumrân* 18: 373–96.

MacGregor, Neil. 2014. *Germany: Memories of a Nation*. London: Allen Lane.

Maier, Johann, and Kurt Schubert. 1973. *Die Qumran-Essener: Texte der Schriftrollen und Lebensbild der Gemeinde*. 2nd edn 1982; 3rd edn 1992. München: Ernst Reinhardt Verlag.

Maier, Johann. 1978. *Die Tempelrolle vom Toten Meer*. München: Ernst Reinhardt Verlag.

Maier, Johann. 1995. *Die Qumran-Essener: Die Texte vom Toten Meer*. Bd. I–III. First edn, 1960. München: Ernst Reinhardt Verlag.

McCarthey, Carmel. 2007. *Deuteronomy*. Biblia Hebraica Quinta 5. Stuttgart: Deutsche Bibelgesellschaft.

Newsom, Carol A. *Songs of the Sabbath Sacrifice: A Critical Edition*. Harvard Semitic Studies 27. Atlanta: Scholars Press, 1985.

Nicholson, Ernest W. 1998. *The Pentateuch in the Twentieth Century: The Legacy of Julius Wellhausen*. Oxford: Clarendon Press.

Noth, Martin. 1951. "Eine Bemerkung zur Jesajarolle vom Toten Meer." *Vetus Testamentum* 1: 224–26.

Osten-Sacken, Peter von der. 1969. *Gott und Belial: traditionsgeschichtliche Untersuchungen zum Dualismus in den Texten aus Qumran*. Studien zur Umwelt des Neuen Testaments 6. Göttingen: Vandenhoeck & Ruprecht.

Rabin, Ira. 2016. "Material Analysis of the Fragments." Pp. 61–77 in *Gleanings from the Caves: Dead Sea Scrolls and Artefacts from the Schøyen Collection*. Ed. Torleif Elgvin, Kipp Davis and Michael Langlois. Library of Second Temple Studies 71. London: Bloomsbury T&T Clark.

Rohrhirsch, Ferdinand. 1996. *Wissenschaftstheorie und Qumran: Die Geltungsbegründungen von Aussagen in der Biblischen Archäologie am Beispiel von Chirbet Qumran und En Feschcha*. Novum Testamentum et Orbis Antiquus 32. Freiburg: Universitätsverlag; Göttingen: Vandenhoeck & Ruprecht.

Römer, Thomas. 2013. "Zwischen Urkunden, Fragmenten und Ergänzungen: Zum Stand der Pentateuchforschung." *Zeitschrift für die alttestamentliche Wissenschaft* 125: 2–24.

Sander, Ruth, and Kerstin Mayerhofer. 2010. *Retrograde Hebrew and Aramaic Dictionary*. Journal for Ancient Judaism Supplement 1. Göttingen: Vandenhoeck & Ruprecht.

Schick, Alexander, with Otto Betz and Frank M. Cross. 1996. *Jesus und die Schriftrollen von Qumran: Wurde die Bibel verfälscht?* Westerland/Sylt: Schwengeler Verlag und A. Schick Bibelausstellung Sylt.

———, with Uwe Gleßmer. 2000. *Auf der Suche nach der Urbibel. Die Schriftrollen vom Toten Meer, das Alte Testament und der geheime Bibelcode*. Wuppertal: Oncken Verlag.

Simmel, Georg. 1907. "Die Ruine: Ein ästhetischer Versuch." *Der Tag* 96 (22. Februar).

Smend, Rudolf. 1999. "Wellhausen, Julius (1844–1918)." Pp. 629–31 in *Dictionary of Biblical Interpretation*. Ed. John H. Hayes. 2 vols. Nashville, TN: Abingdon Press.

———. 2004. *Julius Wellhausen: Ein Bahnbrecher in drei Disziplinen*. Carl Friedrich von Siemens Stiftung, Themen Band 84. München: Carl Friedrich von Siemens Stiftung.

Stegemann, Hartmut. 1963. *Rekonstruktion der Hodajot. Ursprüngliche Gestalt und kritisch bearbeiteter Text der Hymnenrolle aus Höhle 1 von Qumran*. PhD diss., University of Heidelberg.

———. 1971. *Die Entstehung der Qumrangemeinde*. Bonn.

———. 1992. "The Qumran Essenes–Local Members of the Main Jewish Union in Late Second Temple Times." Pp. 83–166 in *The Madrid Qumran Congress: Proceedings of the International Congress on the Dead Sea Scrolls, Madrid 18–21 March 1991*. Ed. Julio Trebolle Barrera and Luis Vegas Montaner. Studies on the Texts of the Desert of Judah 11. Leiden: Brill/Madrid: Universidad Complutense.

———, 1993. *Die Essener, Qumran, Johannes der Täufer und Jesus*. Freiburg im Breisgau: Herder. ET: *The Library of Qumran: On the Essenes, Qumran, John the Baptist, and Jesus*. Grand Rapids, MI: Eerdmans, 1998.

———, with Eileen Schuller. 2009. *Qumran Cave 1.III: 1QHodayot^a with Incorporation of 1QHodayot^b and 4QHodayot^{a-f}*. Discoveries in the Judaean Desert 40. Oxford: Clarendon Press.

Steudel, Annette. 1994. *Der Midrasch zur Eschatologie aus der Qumrangemeinde (4QMidrEschat$^{a.b}$). Materielle Rekonstruktion, Textbestand, Gattung und traditionsgeschichtliche Einordnung des durch 4Q174 ("Florilegium") und 4Q177 ("Catena A") repräsentierten Werkes aus den Qumranfunden*. Studies on the Texts of the Desert of Judah 13. Leiden: Brill.

———, Editor. 2001. *Die Texte aus Qumran II: Hebräisch/Aramäisch und Deutsch*. Darmstadt: Wissenschaftliche Buchgesellschaft.

————. 2012. "Basic Research, Methods and Approaches to the Qumran Scrolls in German-Speaking Countries." Pp. 565–99 in *The Dead Sea Scrolls in Scholarly Perspective: A History of Research*. Ed. Devorah Dimant. Studies on the Texts of the Desert of Judah 99. Leiden: Brill.

Stökl Ben Ezra, Daniel. 2016. *Qumran: Die Texte vom Toten Meer und das antike Judentum*. Jüdische Studien 3; Uni-Taschenbuch 4681. Tübingen: Mohr Siebeck.

Thiede, Carsten Peter. 1986. *Die älteste Evangelien-Handschrift? Das Markus-Fragment von Qumran und die Anfänge der schriftlichen Überlieferung des Neuen Testaments*. Wuppertal: Brockhaus.

————. 2002. *Die Messias-Sucher: Die Schriftrollen vom Toten Meer und die jüdischen Ursprünge des Christentums*. Stuttgart: Kreuz Verlag.

Tov, Emanuel. 2005. *Scribal Practices and Approaches Reflected in the Texts Found in the Judean Desert*. Studies on the Texts of the Desert of Judah 54. Leiden: Brill.

Trebolle Barrera, Julio. 1995. "54. 4QKgs." Pp. 171–83 in *Qumran Cave 4.IX: Deuteronomy, Joshua, Judges, Kings*. Ed. Eugene Ulrich and Frank Moore Cross. Discoveries in the Judaean Desert 14. Oxford: Clarendon Press.

VanderKam, James C. 1998. *Einführung in die Qumranforschung: Geschichte und Bedeutung der Schriften vom Toten Meer*. Uni-Taschenbuch. Göttingen: Vandenhoeck & Ruprecht.

Waal, Edmund de. 2015. *The White Road: A Pilgrimage of Sorts*. London: Chatto & Windus.

Wacholder, Ben-Zion, and Martin G. Abegg. 1991. *A Preliminary Edition of the Unpublished Dead Sea Scrolls: The Hebrew and Aramaic Texts from Cave Four. Fascicle One*. Washington, DC: Biblical Archaeology Society.

Wacholder, Ben-Zion, and Martin G. Abegg. 1992. *A Preliminary Edition of the Unpublished Dead Sea Scrolls: The Hebrew and Aramaic Texts from Cave Four. Fascicle Two*. Washington, DC: Biblical Archaeology Society.

Wacholder, Ben-Zion, and Martin G. Abegg. 1995. *A Preliminary Edition of the Unpublished Dead Sea Scrolls: The Hebrew and Aramaic Texts from Cave Four. Fascicle Three*. Washington, DC: Biblical Archaeology Society.

Wacholder, Ben-Zion, Martin G. Abegg and James Bowley. 1996. *A Preliminary Edition of the Unpublished Dead Sea Scrolls: The Hebrew and Aramaic Texts from Cave Four. Fascicle Four: Concordance of Fascicles 1–3*. Washington, DC: Biblical Archaeology Society.

Wellhausen, Julius. 1885. *Prolegomena to the History of Israel with a Reprint of the Article* Israel *from the "Encyclopedia Britannica"*. Edinburgh: Adam & Charles Black. [Trans. from German 1883 edn]

Xeravits, Géza G., and Peter Porzig. 2015. *Einführung in die Qumran-Literatur: Die Handschriften vom Toten Meer*. Studium. Berlin: de Gruyter.